ADHD

The SEN series

Able, Gifted and Talented – Janet Bates and
  Sarah Munday
Dyspraxia – Geoff Brookes
Profound and Multiple Learning Difficulties –
  Corinna Cartwright and Sarah Wind-Condie
ADHD – Fintan O'Regan
*Surviving and Succeeding in Special Educational
  Needs* – Fintan O'Regan
Visual Needs – Olga Miller and Adam Ockelford
Language and Communication Difficulties –
  Dimitra Hartas
Dyslexia – Gavin Reid
Emotional and Behavioural Difficulties – Roy Howarth
  and Pam Fisher

ADHD

Fintan J. O'Regan MA (Management)

continuum
LONDON • NEW YORK

Continuum International Publishing Group
The Tower Building
11 York Road
London
SE1 7NX

15 East 26th Street
New York, NY 10010

www.continuumbooks.com

British Library Cataloguing-in-Publication Data
A catalogue record for this book is available from the British Library.

ISBN: 0 8264 7613 9 (paperback)

Typeset by Servis Filmsetting Ltd, Manchester
Printed and bound in Great Britain by MPG Books Ltd, Bodmin,
Cornwall

Contents

Foreword

This is a handbook for all teachers dealing with Attention Deficit Hyperactivity Disorder (ADHD) and its associated conditions. Its main aim is to provide teachers with up-to-date information and to demonstrate a variety of ways in which they can play a proactive role in helping both children and young adults.

Chapter 1 considers what ADHD actually is, while Chapter 2 outlines the tremendous impact that ADHD and related learning difficulties have not only on the individuals themselves but on schools, families and society in general. Chapter 3 considers the educational implications of ADHD, and strategies and solutions for more effective learning are outlined in some detail. Chapter 4 considers a range of behaviour management options to assist the process of successful child development.

Chapter 5 considers the implications of the many socialization problems experienced by children with ADHD, especially with regard to peers, siblings and parents. Finally, Chapter 6 considers ADHD as a multi-agency process and includes information on medication and on what may lie in store for the future.

Introduction

When I was a young teacher working in Newcastle upon Tyne in the 1980s, dealing with children with behaviour issues seemed quite straightforward. Either they did what you asked them to do or you put them in detention. There were always one or two students I used to feel sorry for as they did not seem to understand why they always got themselves into trouble. And it appeared to me and some of the other staff that they were not being deliberately disruptive but that they were not in control of themselves.

Not having heard of dyslexia at that time, let alone attention deficit hyperactivity disorder (ADHD), clearly I did not understand why certain students acted the way they did.

At this time my main approach to classroom management was that of my Head of Department, a man called Bill Thompson, whose advice was: 'Get 'em in; Get on with it; Get on with them; Get 'em out.'

Over the years I have found this approach very helpful, although I might add that in dealing with students who exhibit learning and behavioural problems I have tended to try to 'Get on with them' before 'Getting on with it'.

Having subsequently worked as a teacher in the USA

and then in a London special needs school, my introduction into the key topic of this book was in 1988,
when a mother explained to me that people in the UK
did not accept the term ADD and that nobody understood the effect that 'attention devastation disorder'
was having on her life.

Being familiar with the full term ADHD by this time,
I thought she was making a bit of a joke, but when I
looked at her again I saw she was not. This in fact was
the impact that her child was having on her life and on
the rest of the family.

Since then, both in my position as a headmaster
of a specialist school for children aged seven to
eighteen and as an LEA advisor to a number of mainstream schools and special schools, I have worked
with hundreds of children with ADHD and related
conditions.

Also, in my role as a presenter and trainer I have
worked with teachers and staff in related multi-
agencies throughout the UK and Ireland. We have come
to the conclusion that no 'off-the-shelf' solutions are
available and that every child with ADHD is different.

In all the time I have spent working with individual
children, colleagues and parents, one thing has
become very clear: ADHD is clearly a condition that can
'devastate' the hopes, dreams and aspirations of not
only the individuals with ADHD themselves but also
those around them.

Having said this, with the proper understanding,
acceptance and recognition of the ADHD condition so
much can be achieved. I have been truly honoured to
have worked with some remarkable professionals and
parents whose commitment to finding solutions to

behaviour issues have resulted in many individuals with ADHD leading successful and fulfilling lives.

The D for 'devastation' in the story above could also have stood for many other Ds: Despair, Disillusionment, Defiance, Destructive, Difficult, etc.; but D also stands for Diagnosis, Determination and Desire.

It is with the positive Ds that we will attempt in this book to discover how to realize the impact of ADHD and consider a number of intervention approaches to help individuals with this condition to fulfil their potential within the school community.

As Bill Thompson would also say, there are 'no short cuts to anywhere worth going'. The journey a child with ADHD must travel alongside those individuals assigned to help them, though often frustrating, can also be a lot of fun.

Children with ADHD need us to help them help themselves.

1

Information about ADHD

What is ADHD?

Attention deficit hyperactivity disorder, more commonly known as ADHD, is a complex and often controversial term. It is an internationally validated medical condition, involving brain dysfunction, in which individuals have difficulty in controlling impulses, inhibiting their behaviour and sustaining their attention span. This leads to a variety of educational, behavioural, social and related difficulties.

ADHD often overlaps with other conditions such as dyslexia, dyspraxia and oppositional defiant disorder (ODD). The impact of this will be discussed further in Chapter 2.

The core features of ADHD are:

♦ poor attention span

♦ excessive impulsivity

♦ hyperactivity.

Symptoms of poor attention span may include:

♦ disorganization

♦ forgetfulness

♦ being easily distracted

♦ difficulty in sustaining attention in tasks or play activities.

Symptoms of hyperactive or impulsive behaviours may include:

♦ fidgeting

♦ having trouble playing quietly

♦ interrupting others

♦ always being on the go.

While we all display such behaviours from time to time, the difference in those with ADHD is the degree and intensity with which they occur. ADHD is a chronic disorder, which can begin in infancy and can extend through adulthood. It can have negative affects on a child's life at school, at home and in his or her community.

The History of ADHD

ADHD was first identified in 1902 by Professor Still in his studies of a group of children who showed an 'abnormal incapacity for sustained attention, restlessness and fidgetiness'. He discovered that the children had serious deficiencies in 'volitional inhibition' of a biological origin. His belief that the disorder was caused by something 'within' the child and not by environmental factors received further support from the chance discovery by Bradley (1937) that the psycho-stimulant amphetamine could reduce levels of hyperactivity and behavioural problems. As a result, the term 'minimal brain damage' or 'minimal brain dysfunction' were used until the late 1950s. At this point the emphasis shifted from aetiology to behavioural expression, and hyperactivity became the defining feature.

The process of analysing the symptoms as a means of explaining the syndrome was upheld by a number of influential researchers. They believed that attention rather than hyperactivity was the key feature of the condition. As a result 'attention' became the key word. There have since been repeated attempts at reformulating, leading to the current classification in the Fourth Edition of the American Psychiatric Association (DSM IV) in 1994, see page 9.

ADHD Today

Combined Type ADHD

This is diagnosed by the presence to a significant degree of at least six of the nine criteria for attention plus at least six of the nine criteria for hyperactivity-impulsivity. In addition there must be evidence that the symptoms presented themselves before the child reached the age of seven; that symptoms are manifested in at least two different settings; that they result in a significant impairment of the child's academic, occupational and social abilities; and that they cannot be better explained by another psychological or psychiatric condition.

ADHD Inattentive Type + ADHD Hyperactive Impulsive Type

Requires at least six of the nine symptoms for inattention and recognizes that certain individuals may have profound inattentiveness without impulsivity/hyperactivity. This is one of the reasons why in some textbooks you may find ADHD written with a slash – AD/HD. This distinguishes inattentive ADHD from the third type, known as hyperactive/impulsive type, which requires at least six out of the nine symptoms listed in the hyperactive/impulsivity section. ADHD inattentive type refers to children who have greater difficulty with memory and perceptual motor speed and are prone to daydreaming and often socially withdrawn.

Hyperactive/Impulsive Type

Information about ADHD

ADHD Criteria from the DSM IV (1994) (Adapted from the American Psychiatric Association from Diagnostic and Statistical Manual of Mental Disorders 1994)

A1 Inattention. At least six (or more) of the following symptoms of inattention have persisted for at least six months to a degree that is maladaptive and inconsistent with developmental level.

a) Often fails to give close attention to details or makes careless mistakes in schoolwork or other activities.
b) Often has difficulty in sustaining attention in tasks or play activities.
c) Often does not seem to listen when spoken to directly.
d) Often does not follow through on instructions and fails to finish schoolwork, chores or duties in the workplace (not due to oppositional behaviour or failure to understand instructions).
e) Often has difficulty organizing tasks and activities.
f) Often loses things necessary for tasks and activities (e.g. toys, school assignments, pencils, books or tools).
g) Often avoids, dislikes or is reluctant to engage in tasks that require sustained mental effort (such as schoolwork or homework).
h) Is often easily distracted by extraneous stimuli.
i) Is often forgetful in daily activities.

A2 Hyperactivity/Impulsivity. At least six (or more) of the following symptoms of hyperactivity-impulsivity have persisted for at least six months to a degree that is maladaptive and inconsistent with developmental level:

Hyperactivity
a) Often fidgets with hands or feet or squirms in seat.
b) Often leaves seat in classroom or in other situations in which remaining seated is expected.
c) Often runs about or climbs excessively in situations in which it is inappropriate. (In adolescence or adulthood may be limited to subjective feelings of restlessness.)
d) Often has difficulty in playing or engaging in leisure activities quietly.
e) Is often 'on the go' or often acts as if 'driven by a motor'.
f) Often talks excessively.

Impulsivity

g) Often blurts out answers before questions have been completed.
h) Often has difficulty waiting turn.
i) Often interrupts or intrudes on others (e.g. butts into conversations or games).
B   Some hyperactive-impulsiveness or inattentive symptoms that caused impairment were present before the age of seven.
C   Some impairment is present in two or more settings.
D   There must be clinically significant impairment in social, academic or occupational functioning.
E   The symptoms do not occur during the course of PDD, schizophrenia or other psychotic disorder and are not better accounted for by another mental disorder.

Redefining ADHD

Professor Russell Barkley, an eminent ADHD expert, argues that a key element of the ADHD condition is the inability to inhibit behaviour so that the demands for the future can be met. In other words, people with ADHD are drawn to the present: there really is no future or past, just the 'NOW'!

An analogy might be that when you step on a dog's tail it howls. No discussion occurs within the dog's brain, because howling is an instinctive reaction or reflex. No inhibition takes place.

Though no single part of the brain is involved with modulating behaviour, it would appear that the main areas involved in this process are in our frontal and pre-frontal lobes. These frontal lobes consider where we came from, where we want to go, how we control ourselves and how we want to get there. This ability to put on the brakes gives us the luxury of thinking before we speak or act. The lack of control, or inability to apply the brakes, is central to a whole host of issues for the individual with ADHD, including:

♦ self talk

♦ working memory

♦ foresight (planning for the future)

♦ sense of time

♦ shifting agenda

♦ separating emotion from fact.

How Common is ADHD?

Most research indicates that five per cent of the school-age population are affected to some degree by ADHD, and of these approximately one per cent are severely hyperactive. In addition, 30–40 per cent of all children referred for professional help because of behaviour problems come with a presenting complaint associated with ADHD.

While more boys appear to be affected than girls, the ratio of boys to girls is somewhere in the region of 4:1 in both combined and hyperactive/impulsive types. Why this should be the case is open to interpretation, but there is no doubt that boys and girls present the features of ADHD differently. What is more, parents and other adult supervisors respond to their symptoms differently.

However, it is interesting to note that in the inattentive type category the ratio of boys to girls is 1:1. The symptoms are far less obvious than the more demonstrative hyperactive/impulsive type and this may be overlooked and misdiagnosed in many children.

ADHD and Age

There is no age limit for children with ADHD. Although it is often difficult to diagnose in very young children, the effects, often involving difficult behaviour, will be equally demanding for both the individuals and their families. These will be the children who stop getting invitations to birthday parties and are no longer asked over to play after school by their peers, as their behaviour may be unpredictable and even dangerous.

As children grow into teenagers many additional difficulties can arise after years of struggling and failure at school. At this stage, although the hyperactivity might be reduced, the impulsivity, poor attentional skills and oppositional behaviour may well be more apparent. Adult ADHD is also a very real and often disabling condition and can result in a host of difficulties relating to employment and success in relationships with other people.

ADHD and Intelligence

Though ADHD is found at every IQ level, most individuals may be of average or above average intelligence. In fact, ADHD may mask intelligence in gifted children who will show only average or below average performance. Alternatively, high intelligence apparently enables children to cope academically, until some crisis point is reached, often during adolescence. Poor self-esteem and social difficulties often predominate, however.

It needs to be pointed out that a number of environmental factors, together with IQ complications and age of diagnosis, can modify the outlook of those with ADHD. What is more, with a comprehensive approach to management, even those with severe ADHD can usually be helped extremely effectively.

What Causes ADHD?

A 1987 report to the US Congress prepared by the Interagency Committee of Learning Disabilities attributes the probable cause of ADHD to 'abnormalities in neurological function, in particular to disturbance in brain neurochemistry involving a neurological class of neurotransmitters'. Researchers are unclear, however, about the specific mechanisms by which these neurotransmitter chemicals influence attention, impulse control and activity level.

Although many ADHD children tend to develop secondary emotional problems, ADHD in itself may be related to biological factors and is not primarily an emotional disorder. Nevertheless, emotional and behavioural problems can frequently be seen in ADHD children due to problems that these children have at school, at home and in their social environment. Characteristics such as inattentiveness, impulsivity and underachievement can also be found in non-ADHD students who suffer primarily from emotional difficulties, which can effect concentration and effort. These students may have 'motivational' deficits leading to diminished classroom attentiveness and performance. Differential diagnosis is therefore an essential prerequisite to effective treatment.

ADHD

The American writer Michael Gordon sums up the fundamental issues of ADHD as:

The Core Deficit that ADHD children experience is a thick barrier between themselves and life's consequences.

(Michael Gordon, 1991)

This highlights one of the main problems for ADHD sufferers: namely that the condition is often mistaken for something else – the child being uncooperative or plain naughty. Those with ADHD simply do not respond to redirection in the same ways as other children. In many cases the child might start out as enthusiastic but unsuccessful; and then become angry and unsuccessful.

These are the children who could be described as 'consistently inconsistent'. When they are told off by an adult they may appear distracted, or when redirected they may smile or smirk impulsively while being distracted by a movement or another thought that has leapt into their mind. Although this is not always an intentional response it can nevertheless be highly annoying for the supervisor involved. Sometimes these unintentional impulsive thoughts or comments can lead to problems between adults and pupils, such as in the case of Simon outlined below.

Instead of being at homework club after school, 13-year-old Simon was spotted outside on the street on his skateboard. After being asked to come inside and join the others Simon appeared flustered and disorientated and was finding it hard to settle at his desk, and his skateboard kept getting in his way. Simon, though badly disorganized, was usually a passive and generally compliant student. After the fourth minute of watching him struggle to get started, the teacher suggested removing his skateboard until later. It came as a tremendous shock to the teacher when Simon's response was to jump out of his seat in a furious temper, yelling, 'If you do that you'll be sorry!'

The room became filled with a deadly hush, apart from one child who whispered, 'Oh dear, Simon is in for it now'.

It is important to remember that children with ADHD will not always be inattentive or easily distracted. In fact, they can sometimes be over-focused. As Michael Gordon states:

> Their behaviour will vary according to the degree to which rules are managed, the amount of structure and support for compliance and the degree to which the child is interested in the activity.
>
> *(Michael Gordon, 1991)*

This is so very true. Once pupils with ADHD are engaged in something in which they have an interest, or that someone has made interesting for them, they can be productive and successful. Having said that, the impact of ADHD when the behaviour of children is not compliant can be dramatic. It is to this issue that we next turn our attention.

2

Impact of ADHD

It is obviously difficult to assess precisely how much time and money is spent supporting children with ADHD, but one thing is clear: learning difficulties accompanied by behavioural issues are costly. As in most businesses today, the most expensive resource in schools is personnel. Learning and behavioural difficulties engage vast amounts of personnel time in terms of:

♦ specialist teaching (often one-to-one provision)

♦ additional learning support staffing

♦ meetings

♦ conference phone calls

♦ paper administration

♦ communication with external agencies.

To illustrate this, a recent meeting concerning one child took up most of a morning. Eight adults were present, including a Senior LEA Educational Psychologist, a social worker, the child's current head teacher, the classroom teacher, two learning support teachers, the careers advisor and a parent.

ADHD

This is by no means a unique scenario. On a day-to-day basis vast resources are absorbed in planning, managing and teaching children with ADHD.

Within mainstream schools, however, children with ADHD require varying amounts of support depending in part on the nature of their difficulties, the type of school they attend and, to a very large extent, the training of the special educational needs coordinator (SENCO) and the skills, knowledge and attitude of the majority of the regular teaching staff in relation to special educational needs (SEN).

While policies vary widely across the UK, one issue is clear: inclusion means different things in the context of different schools. In some schools, children with ADHD can spend up to 85 per cent of their day in the school's Learning Support Unit, either with the SENCO or with a learning support assistant (LSA) supervised away from their main classroom.

The real question, of course, is the potential cost for schools both in terms of identification of and provision for ADHD. Conservative estimates made by Paul Cooper, Professor of Education at the University of Leicester, put the number of school-age children with ADHD in the UK at approximately 500,000, though fewer than 50,000 students have been diagnosed.

In reality, however, in every class of 30 children it is likely that there will be one or two students with ADHD. Due to the potential impact these children will have on class dynamics in terms of teacher time and social interaction, it could be argued that either directly or indirectly ADHD will affect every student in every classroom in the UK.

There is no doubt that early identification and intervention in teaching and managing students with ADHD can play a huge part in preventing the development of secondary behavioural issues. This philosophy was approved by Estelle Morris, former Minister of Education, who commented in the revised 2001 Code of Practice that 'the focus is on preventative work to ensure that children's special educational needs are identified as quickly as possible and that early action is taken to meet those needs'.

Although many teachers, support staff and administrators are aware of the term ADHD, few see it as a medical disorder rather than a behavioural issue. Teachers at the chalkface have to address the core symptoms of inattention, impulsivity, hyperactivity and often other behavioural or socialization difficulties.

Problems at School

Parents of children with ADHD often have very negative experiences to report. Their main concerns include:

♦ lack of understanding by teachers

♦ confusing and lengthy processes to obtain support through action plans, statementing, etc.

♦ lack of understanding by health care professionals

♦ a feeling of being in the dark and having to cope without support or information.

One particular family's story is unfortunately an all-too-common experience. Their grandson was diagnosed with ADHD at the age of nine and a half. He is currently 15 years old.

Although there were problems at primary level, they were largely contained in a relatively small school (about 200) plus help through statementing. However, he became increasingly disruptive when changes in his routine occurred around the SATs exam time and also in the evenings when his medication had worn off.

We anticipated difficulties on transfer to a large secondary school, as did his head teacher. His single parent mother led a chaotic, disorganized and crisis-led life due to her own recently diagnosed ADHD together with her inability to remember their medications. We tried to get him into a Therapeutic School (Beacon Award-Winning) as a weekly boarder where the problems of his disadvantaged home situation, as well as his educational needs, would be met. The school's emphasis was on the whole person, with psychological intervention designed to help with emotional and behavioural difficulties. We also felt they would be able to monitor his medical treatment for ADHD better than his home situation.

The Local Education Authority (LEA) was not supportive but, following pressure, increased his support. He was placed in a Secondary School with over 1,000 pupils. The school had a very good Special Needs system, but after four terms he was permanently excluded for intimidation. The Educational Psychologist suggested to the Special Education Service that 'now is an appropriate time to consider alternatives, as to place him in yet another mainstream environment or on a possibly limited timetable through Student Support Services will replicate those conditions which have possibly been influential in the escalation of his difficulties.'

For almost three terms he was in an educational state of limbo, eventually getting five half-days a week in a Special Needs Teaching Support Service (who had no literature or training on ADHD), before transfer to an EBD school. We initially visited the school and expressed our concerns regarding adequate specialized provision.

Unfortunately our fears have again been justified and following several lengthy suspensions he is awaiting re-acceptance at the school. There has been no provision for anger management and currently it is his paediatrician who is looking to arrange this for him.

Our impression is that the LEA has not met its education obligations and has tactically stalled over the years until our grandson has reached the age of fifteen, which is too late to meet his needs at this stage.

What Parents Want

Most parents want their children to stay in mainstream schools if at all possible, but they do realize that teachers are unfortunately often too busy and pressurized to cope. Awareness of ADHD remains low, and special provision is generally made only as a response to parents' perseverance and stubbornness.

That ADHD has a significant impact on the lives of

individuals themselves and their families is in no doubt, especially when we consider some of the main effects of this condition:

♦ lack of foresight/hindsight, i.e. always living for the moment

♦ poor organizational skills, complete lack of time management

♦ lack of social skills and inability to read social clues

♦ poor frustration tolerance, being inflexible

♦ risk-taking/thrill-seeking behaviours

♦ problems with transitions, problems in paying attention to others

♦ lying, swearing, stealing and blaming others.

It should be said, however, that not all individuals will manifest all these traits and that any potential impact of these characteristics will be dramatically affected by the support of parents and the options for management that are available. Having said that, the risk factors for unsocial and unhappy individuals are significantly increased if some or all of these traits exist.

Further evidence of the potential impact of ADHD comes from data prepared by Professor Russell Barkley, currently the foremost world expert in the field of ADHD, on how children with ADHD compare with other children. These are the results of three studies (1997) on general behaviour patterns, exclusions from school and sexual activity.

General Behaviour Patterns	ADHD Children (%)	Typical Children (%)
Argues with adults	72	21
Blames others for own mistakes	66	17
Acts touchy or is easily annoyed	71	20
Swears	40	6
Lies	49	5
Stealing (not involving threats)	50	7
Exclusions	ADHD Children (%)	Control (%)
Temporarily excluded	60	18
Permanently excluded	14	5
Completed school	67	100
Sexual Activity	ADHD Children (%)	Control (%)
Number of Partners	18.5	6.5
Birth control used	76	91
Sexually transmitted disease	17	4
Pregnancies	41	4
Children sired	38	1
Children not in parental care	52	–

As each of these three categories demonstrates, the low probability that individuals with ADHD will achieve success in the school environment and/or in relationships with other people can have a dramatic impact not just on the lives of these individuals and their families but on society as a whole.

Co-morbidity of ADHD

In order to diagnose ADHD correctly, an awareness is required of the range of disorders that may often accompany it or be mistaken for it. Specific learning difficulties such as dyslexia, dyspraxia and dyscalculia occur in approximately 40 per cent of children with ADHD, while disruptive behavioural disorders such as oppositional defiant disorder (ODD) and conduct disorder occur in about 50 per cent of cases. Anxiety disorders occur in about 30 per cent of all ADHD individuals.

Many of these labels can themselves be confusing, and indeed we appear to have a whole range of ways of describing why children can't or won't learn. The key terms mentioned above can be found in the appendices at the back of this book.

What statistics can't tell us is the range of social and physiological elements that can have a direct impact on the life of someone with ADHD. One way of assessing this is to look at the potential pathway for an ADHD individual within the school environment:

Age 7	Key Stage 2	low self-esteem
Age 11	Key Stage 3	disruptive behaviour, learning delay, poor social skills
Age 14	Key Stage 4	ODD, challenging behaviour, criminal behaviour, school exclusion, substance abuse, conduct disorder, lack of motivation, complex learning difficulties

Although not all individuals will follow this path, it is all too often the net result for a child who is not diagnosed or recognized within the school system. In many cases it could be summed up in the sequence, 'Can't Learn, Won't Learn, Don't Care'.

Ivan was having a typical day. He just couldn't keep still and kept fiddling with a pen, which once taken away by the teacher was replaced with an elastic band. This was flicked across the room and struck

Sadie across the face. 'Oh,' she cried, 'Ivan, you shouldn't have done that', as she stood up yelling in the middle of the class. The teacher Mr Flynn had had enough of this and of Year 8C in general. 'Out,' he said to Ivan, 'off to the LSU. Go and see Ms Parker.' Ivan didn't mind too much as he quite liked Ms Parker and preferred the sanctuary of the Learning Support Unit to the classroom anyway.

As he left the classroom he saw Mark and as he walked past him whispered something in his ear. This caused Mark to fly out of his seat and to follow Ivan out of the classroom. The two of them began pummelling each other in the corridor. Before Mr Flynn could move, five other students rushed out of the classroom to watch the action. Mr Flynn rushed out and pulled the two boys apart, Ivan laughing and Mark spluttering, 'he cussed my mother, Sir'.

It may appear quite dramatic to say that ADHD can result in criminal behaviour – there are many other causes, of course, such as social disintegration, lack of parental control and lack of discipline in schools. A brief look at the data collated by the Youth Justice Board in their 2003 report shows some interesting patterns.

♦ Only 30 per cent of young offenders were with both parents

♦ 27 per cent had previous permanent exclusions

♦ 41 per cent were truanting regularly

♦ 42 per cent were rated as underachieving at school

- ◆ 40 per cent were associated with peers actively involved in criminal activity

- ◆ 25 per cent had friends who were all offenders

- ◆ 50 per cent were recorded as having used cannabis

- ◆ 75 per cent were considered to be impulsive and to act without thinking

- ◆ Nine per cent were considered to be at risk of self-harm or suicide (15 per cent in the case of females).

The most interesting statistic is that 75 per cent of offenders were considered to be impulsive and to act without thinking. These are key symptoms of ADHD, where sufferers often act in a disruptive, defiant and sometimes dangerous way, taking risks wherever possible. As one experienced teacher explains, 'they think about it, but it's too late – they have already done it'.

The police are in no doubt that ADHD is a legitimate term and explains a great deal of low-level offending.

Diagnosing ADHD

As we have already seen, ADHD occurs in combination with other issues; issues that can ultimately mask ADHD. This means that correct diagnosis of ADHD is vital. The diagnosis can only be made, however, by ruling out other factors related to medical, emotional or environmental variables that could cause similar symptoms. Therefore physicians, psychologists and educators should conduct a multidisciplinary evaluation of the child, which would include:

♦ medical studies

♦ psychological and educational testing

♦ speech and language assessment

♦ neurological evaluation

♦ behavioural rating scales completed by the child's parents and teachers.

This process should also include the following:

♦ medical evaluation

♦ parent interview

♦ teacher interview

♦ rating scales

♦ computerized testing

♦ achievement testing

♦ intellectual testing.

Assessment Procedures

In order to make a proper assessment of the child, it is necessary to consider the child's symptoms from three perspectives – those of the parent, the school and the child.

Parents

♦ Careful interview (review of symptoms, developmental history, signs of parental depression and other effects of child's symptoms on parents)

- Child behaviour checklist or Conner's Rating Scale
- Home situations questionnaire
- Developmental history form
- Locke-Wallace Marital Adjustments Survey

Child

- Interview
- IQ screening
- Gordon Diagnostic System (GDS)
- Achievement test
- Review of school testing
- Observation of parent-child interaction

School

- Discussion with teachers
- Classroom observation
- Teacher rating form or Conner's Rating Scale
- Kendall-Wilcox Behaviour Rating Scale

Once testing is complete the next stage is to consider the results and of course the impact that they may have on the individual and those around them. Although it may seem simplistic, we may consider the impact of ADHD in three main areas – the educational, behavioural and social aspects of the child's life. The way a child with ADHD presents will depend on a number of factors related to age and to the particular profile of difficulties. Some of these areas are listed below:

Educational Impact

♦ Cannot get started

♦ Underachieves

♦ Works too slowly/quickly

♦ Forgets instructions/explanations

♦ Off task, lazy

♦ Always leaves things to the last minute

♦ Easily distracted

♦ Procrastinates

♦ Poor motivation, easily frustrated

♦ Difficulty in completing tasks

♦ Avoids, disorganized

Behavioural Impact

♦ Demanding

♦ Interferes with others

♦ Easily frustrated

♦ Lacks self-control

♦ Restless/fidgety

♦ Talks more than others

♦ Bossy, volatile

ADHD

♦ Disruptive, accident-prone

♦ Easily distracted, has good and bad days

Social Impact

♦ Selfish, egocentric

♦ Anxious, rude, insensitive

♦ Immature, depressed

♦ Low self-esteem

♦ Loud/quiet, boisterous

♦ Thoughtless

♦ Withdrawn

♦ Is without feeling

♦ Doesn't take turns

Although these are not exclusive categories, we will now turn our attention to each in turn and consider them in some detail in the next three chapters.

3

Intervention: Educational Options

Although it is often interpreted as a behavioural term, it is perhaps more appropriate to consider ADHD as difficulty in learning to follow instructions. Although, of course, the impact of ADHD in the home environment is significant, it is often in the school setting that the core features of being impulsive, lack of concentration and being hyperactive are most unhelpful, especially in the group dynamic.

As I mentioned in the last chapter, children with ADHD will not always exhibit the same core symptoms. Whether they do or not will depend on whether they are interested in the task and on the amount of structure and support they receive. However, an equally important element in creative strategies is to enable these 'non-traditional learning children' to access the curriculum. The first step will always be the attitude of the teacher or supervisor to working with students who are often perceived as difficult and disruptive.

The lesson objective was 'Making alternative clocks' for a group of Year 4 students who included Jimmy McNally. This involved the use of candles, water, sand, straws and a whole array of other materials.

Jimmy was one of the students who had to be carefully supervised and was known as a 'problem child'. He did not have any friends in the class and because he had little empathy for his actions was not popular amongst staff. He was often impulsive and hyperactive and could be disruptive and sometimes verbally abusive to both peers and teachers.

On paper, the lesson plan for making 'alternative clocks' appeared faultless and after a lengthy sermon to the students on the issue of health and safety the stage was set. Not long after the lesson began the first problem observed was that Tommy Craig's well-constructed water tower was inadvertently knocked over by Jimmy as he tried to create some extra room for his ever-expanding sand clock design. This led to a confrontation between an understandably aggrieved Tommy and Jimmy. The latter tried to defend his actions by saying that his construction 'needed more room'.

As the lesson moved on my attention was drawn to Daisy Foster's science book, which was now smouldering after Jimmy had tried to move her candle clock down the table away from his project as his construction began to take on skyscraper proportions.

Meanwhile Tom Jeffers' salt timer continued to pour furiously through the end of his now missing bottom section (borrowed by Jimmy) for his 'Trump Tower' sand clock. By now Daisy Foster and Tommy Craig were helping Jimmy as were a number of other pupils to supply extra layers of material in a highly collaborative team effort.

At the end of a tiring yet successful lesson, Jimmy

> McNally rushed up to me as he left the room with his face streaked with grit, his hair soaking wet, shirt and tie hanging off him and said, 'Thanks, Sir, this is the best lesson I've ever had'.

From that day forward the teacher never had a major problem with Jimmy in class and whenever practical or project work was undertaken this previously unpopular individual had any number of pupils who wanted to be in his group.

Inclusion: Overall Principles

One of the 'hot' debates in education recently has been the issue of inclusive schooling. How inclusive should schools be with regard to students who have major issues in contrast to traditional learners?

Inclusion has many definitions. Essentially it concerns every student's entitlement to personal, social and intellectual development. Students should be given an opportunity to achieve their potential. In order to do this, educational systems should be designed to take wide diversities into account, and those with exceptional learning needs and/or disabilities should have access to high-quality and appropriate education.

Although these principles are worthy they are difficult to achieve in practice. This is mainly due to the problem of the resources that are needed to provide for an ever-increasing band of complex difficulties in a traditional classroom.

As a result, teachers and administrators face criticism from all sides about how far specific children should be included in traditional classrooms and, indeed, whether it's correct for them to be included at all. For children with ADHD this is a key debate, as these children will require a variety of options that may be beyond the budget or perhaps outside the culture of the school.

It is perhaps useful to consider, in terms of teaching, how the ADHD child contrasts with a traditional child. The following diagram illustrates this.

Traditional Student

ADHD

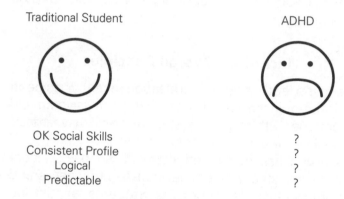

OK Social Skills   ?
Consistent Profile   ?
Logical   ?
Predictable   ?

Needs of the ADHD Child

In essence, the key factors for children with ADHD are clearly specified rules, expectations and instructions. In addition, they need immediate and consistent feedback on behaviour and redirection to task. Reasonable and meaningful consequences for both compliance and non-compliance will also be necessary. Finally, they will need adults who will deal with their problems in a way that is based on knowledge, compassion and respect.

Key rules should be devised in order of seriousness. An example of a priority schedule for secondary students is as follows:

1. Completing work and tasks.

2. No physical or verbal aggression to others.

3. Following school policy (e.g. on use of mobile phones, etc.).

4. No eating or drinking in class.

5. Timekeeping.

6. Adhering to the uniform or dress code (if there is one).

These are the six key rules that in my opinion all students, including those with ADHD, should observe and I would suggest little or no compromise on the above issues, especially the one relating to verbal or physical aggression. If a child cannot or will not try to avoid physically or verbally assaulting another pupil or staff member then that child should lose his or her right to be in that class. Where some flexibility could exist is with issues of calling out, fooling about, fidgeting and organizational skills. There may even be some flexibility towards non-directed and non-aggressive use of bad language, depending on the culture of the school.

With younger students the key rules are more likely to be based on social skills. They will need to be initially limited to a small and definite number and to be made as specific as possible.

Rules should be devised by following a stage-type process, which involves the following:

Stage 1: agree on the rules with the students. Lay out what the consequences are for non-adherence and what rewards are given for observance.

Stage 2: gain commitment from parents/home supervisors.

Stage 3: review and reconsider the rules.

Having established the base camp in terms of laying out a framework for learning, we will now need to consider the options available to assist in some of the other factors that delay this process. We'll consider these under the following headings: dealing with activity level; improving attention span; and impulse control.

Dealing with activity level

Whether it concerns controlling their body or their mind, the child with ADHD appears unable to control their motion as other children do.

Teaching them to do this can be difficult, but strategies do exist. They can be fun as well.

One technique to help younger children sit still is playing statues. The child sits like a statue for a specified time, which can be increased and shown on a bar chart or rewarded by stickers, etc. In essence this process is about focusing the child and helping them to control their bodies, and as a self-taught system it is much more likely to provide a long-term solution to increased activity level. Played alongside a stopwatch and recorded in terms of a visual presentation it can provide long-term benefits in improving activity level.

Variations on this involve playing games called Catch Me if You Can and Beat the Clock, which impose a limit on extraneous movement and focus tasks against a set of expectations for working in the classroom or an activity set against a timed upper limit. (For more information on similar activites, see the Further Resources section of this book.)

With older students, we need to aim for a much

longer period of sustained, controlled activity level (which could be called endurance training), such as lengthening the time and improving the skills in sitting still in a variety of settings. As a result the child will often need to have the session broken down for them, such as in the following example from a 40-minute lesson.

To sit still during the 5/10 introduction to the lesson – teacher indicates part 1 is over.

To focus on the task until the group discussion – teacher indicates part 2 is over.

To get through the group discussion – teacher indicates part 3 is over.

To keep it together during the clear-up time – teacher indicates part 4 is nearly over.

All these games or techniques to harness activity level will need to be practised. Feedback on pupils' success and failure in the initial trials will be crucial in determining long-term outcomes.

Improving attention span

Although being hyperactive and impulsive is not helpful it is without a doubt the issue of poor attention span that is the most damaging feature for children with ADHD, and lengthening this will be the most vital issue in long-term educational success.

The first step is to realize that we cannot assume a child understands what paying attention really is, as for some children with ADHD this is not an inherent process.

A series of role-play activities between you and the

child may need to take place. For example, during a taped story you, the supervisor, would exhibit a series of incidents or examples when you did not get to hear or understand what the story was about. In this example, the child would be asked to clarify examples of why you didn't hear the story or to rate your listening skills. In addition it will be necessary to attempt to show how daydreaming works by reading to yourself while the taped story is on. Once again the child rates your performance in a detective-type way.

Once you feel the child understands what is meant by paying attention it is possible to start to teach attention span by timing their performance against a chart or similar visual tool. If the child is younger then you will often have to do the timing for them, but if they are older they should do it themselves.

Attention cards can be devised and put on students' desks: even computerized checks can be made to hook the child into the task at hand. This opportunity to monitor self-performance on a regular basis alongside the work or activity required is a way of distracting the child in a proactive way.

Impulse Control

Of all the symptoms of ADHD, impulsivity is often the most problematic and leads to the significant and often negative impacts described earlier. Once again the first step to management is to explain the concept of impulsivity to a child who responds instinctively to situations and who, though they appear to be a risk-taker in their own eyes, is in fact susceptible to a reflex over which they have little or no control.

Explaining impulsive behaviour may be easier with some students than others, but the best place to start is to consider recent examples of incidents and to determine through the student's own words how these incidents could have been handled differently. Getting the child to consider a number of separate situations and listing an impulsive act versus a thought-out act would be a starting point.

For example:

Impulsive Act	Thought-out Act
Running into street	Pausing at kerb, checking for traffic
Interrupting conversations	Saying 'Excuse me' and waiting your turn

The next stage is to construct a chart with a specific situation and ask the child to clarify what they think the negative consequence would be versus what would be listed as 'Alternative Thought', for example not doing homework.

We need to consider how we can increase the length of time a student takes between thinking and acting.

Again, there will be different ways of teaching this with younger and older kids, but essentially they need to be persuaded that they can be in control of something. In this particular case of their own impulses! However, it is essential to depersonalize the issue and to move it away from themselves and on to specific situations.

In terms of day-to-day classroom management of students with ADHD, some tried and trusted strategies are listed below. In some cases this will simply confirm good practice but as always the key is to be consistent but remain flexible with some of the minor distractions and incidents that will occur.

♦ Seat the student near the teacher but include them as part of the regular class too.

♦ Place the student up front with his/her back to the rest of the class to keep other students out of view.

♦ Surround the ADHD student with good role models, preferably those seen as 'significant others'. Encourage peer tutoring and cooperative learning.

♦ Avoid distracting stimuli. Try not to place the ADHD child near heaters, doors or windows, high-traffic areas, air conditioners.

♦ ADHD children do not handle change well, so avoid transitions, changes in schedule, physical reloca-tion, disruptions. (Monitor closely on field trips.)

♦ Be creative! Produce a 'stimuli-reduced area' for all students to access.

♦ Maintain eye contact with ADHD student during verbal instruction.

♦ Make directions clear and concise. Be consistent with daily instructions.

♦ Simplify complex directions. Avoid multiple com-mands.

♦ Make sure the ADHD student comprehends what they are doing before beginning the task.

- Repeat in a calm, positive manner, if necessary.

- Help the ADHD child to feel comfortable with seeking assistance (most ADHD children won't ask).

- These children need more help for a longer period of time than the average child. Gradually reduce assistance.

- Keep a daily assignment notebook. Make sure the student writes down the assignment and both parents/teachers sign daily for homework tasks.

- Give one task at a time but monitor frequently.

- Modify assignments as necessary. Develop an individualized programme.

- Make sure you are testing knowledge and not attention span.

- Give extra time for certain tasks. The ADHD child may work slowly.

- Keep in mind the ADHD child can easily get frustrated. Stress, pressure and fatigue can break down the child's self-control and lead to poor behaviour.

Specific remedial provision within an individualized education plan (IEP) may also be needed. In addition to addressing difficulties in reading, spelling and mathematics, 40 per cent of children with ADHD also have coexisting issues with dyslexia. It really is the case that on occasions it's not that the child won't learn but that he or she can't learn. As a result they may also need help with:

- written language and creative language

- study skills

- touch typing and laptop skills

- extension reading in maths

- occupational therapy work on fine or gross motor skills

- handwriting

- speech and language therapy

- social skills counselling

- art, music, drama, IT

- use of video/tape recorder.

Depending on the level of literacy and numeracy the approach may entail the use of the LSA or a specialist in dyslexia or other problems.

Materials used may vary in terms of the techniques employed, but there is no doubt that many approaches involve ICT, which appears to be a medium that relates well to the learning process of children with ADHD for the following reasons:

- the ADHD child responds to individualized or one-to-one settings

- attention is focused on the screen

- multi-sensory experience

- non-threatening: can retry problems, constant feed-back and reinforcement

- impersonal: computer doesn't yell or have favourites

- variety of presentation; attend better to novel stimuli

- student can control pace

- flexible: programmed to do many things

- rapid assessment

- game-like approach; challenge.

Literacy and spelling programmes, especially the Active Literacy Kit and Units of Sound, appear particularly effective, along with Word Shark, Number Shark, Text Detective and a host of others on the market (see Further Resources).

Homework

In general it takes at least three times as long for a child with ADHD to do their homework at home than it takes at school. Consequently it is best for the child to do their homework before he or she leaves the school, either in a homework club or at least with a supervisor. At the very least, work should be differentiated (for example multiple choice questions rather than essays) and a second set of books should be kept at home. There can also be a problem with parent involvement at home. I know of one mother who, frustrated by the lack of help she received from her child's school with regard to his homework schedule, sent in the following note to one of his teachers:

Tuesday 7.15 a.m.
Dear Ms Brown
I am spending over two hours a night on Jason's home-work. Please find his laundry enclosed.

Finally, for Key Stage and GCSE examinations a whole host of special arrangements exist for students with ADHD. Although it is important to be aware of these, and to apply for them in advance, the key is practising the options requested. Working with a reader, for example, is a skilled technique and there will need to be at least three or four trials before the student attempts the exam.

Current special arrangement options are as follows:

♦ time allowance

♦ rest periods

♦ use of readers

♦ amanuensis

♦ word processors

♦ spelling, punctuation and grammar.

There are no easy educational solutions for students with ADHD. Every teacher will attempt to find their own strategy in delivering the curriculum and will find a host of ways of presenting the material and getting their students to complete tasks.

The key is to keep trying to find new and different ways to encourage students whose attention may be drawn to any number of other things. Having said this, the main target is that in every class the teacher, as outlined by Sue Cowley in *Getting the Buggers to Behave 2*, must follow the following programme:

> This is the work you must do
> This is the work you should do
> This is the work you could do.

'Must' must *mean* 'must' and there should be no compromises. Failure to comply means that the student's right to attend the class could well be revised.

Educating a child with ADHD can be a difficult and demanding process but also an extremely fulfilling one. Once the child is engaged and interested in the learning process, they are obviously much less likely to engage in other activities that would be regarded as poor or inappropriate behaviour, to which we turn in the next chapter.

4

Intervention: Behavioural Options

Ding Dong Bell
Pussy's in the well.
Ding Dong Bell
Pussy's in the well.
Who put her in?
Little Tommy Fin.
Who pulled her out?
Little Tommy Sprout.
What a naughty boy was that
To try to drown poor pussy cat
Who ne'er did any harm
And killed all the mice
In his father's barn.

Anonymous

Most nursery rhymes originate from specific events in the past and most of them would appear to be about serious issues, for example 'Ring a Ring o' Roses' was about the effect of the Great Plague and 'Jack and Jill' was based on the tale of two young lovers who met tragic deaths on a hill in Hampshire.

Could it be that Master Tommy Fin was acting hyperactively or impulsively when he decided to lower 'poor pussy cat' down the well? Why, indeed, did he do this?

ADHD

Was it an act of wanton naughtiness? Or perhaps the result of an inventive mind seeking to know how much the bucket would carry and how much faster it would descend with its feline cargo? Our experimenter, of course, would conduct his scientific test without regard to the consequences or the trouble it would cause. Perhaps the rhyme served as a warning about the way some children behave. Maybe our nursery rhyme writer was the first-ever child psychologist and blissfully unaware of their diagnosis of ADD.

Behaviour management strategies for children who are defiant, disruptive and difficult are presented in many ways and in many different publications. Everyone is searching for answers about how to deal with this issue.

For children with ADHD the principles of classroom management are as mentioned earlier:

1. Get 'em in.

2. Get on with 'em.

3. Get 'em working.

4. Get 'em out.

Sounds simple, doesn't it? But in practice, the process of doing this with some students can seem impossible. Also, though it is possible not to argue with 1 and 4, specific teachers may want to emphasize 'get 'em working' before 'get on with 'em'. For students with ADHD, however, I would strongly recommend the sequence above.

The reason for this is that two main things will

engage students with ADHD and prevent behavioural issues from occurring. These are: 1) if they are interested in what they doing; and 2) if they are attracted to somebody or something in the context of the task they are being asked to perform.

Obviously, it is impossible to create a specific curriculum that will be interesting to the extent that students who are highly distractible and/or impulsive and hyperactive will be engaged all the time. The question is therefore how we can make the issue of positive behaviour attractive to students with ADHD so they can become interested in either the rewards for complying or concerned about the sanctions for noncompliance.

Not following rules is, of course, one of the major complaints of adults who work with students with ADHD, who appear to have no regard for any rules at all, from not rushing out into the road to sitting still in the classroom. As in the case of some of the issues discussed in the last chapter, understanding why students with ADHD appear to disregard rules is the key to implementing strategies to deal with it.

The key element in teaching rule-governed behaviour management is to limit the rules to the key areas of basic health and safety issues and basic black/white instructions, such as on uniform and time-keeping.

Another factor is to be as specific as possible. It will also be necessary to use multiple prompts to get the rule training operating and to provide immediate feedback on the outcome. What is more, reinforcing the rules with consistent use of positive (and negative) logical consequences will be required.

If we accept the core symptoms, then it is possible to argue that ADHD students are not rule-breakers; they just cannot filter out the demands of environmental stimuli, all of which are priorities for their attention. This is unlike traditional learners who can, for example, ignore a chair being scraped behind them if the teacher is talking to them. In stark contrast, the ADHD child will check out who is making the noise, unless the subject being discussed has a particular interest for them.

As a result, in the mind of an ADHD child each thing in their environment is equally important. They must be trained to prioritize where to focus their attention at given times of the day. Children with ADHD will need to be helped to beat the distractions that take their attention away from the rules of engagement.

Teaching the child with ADHD to overcome distractions is not an impossible task, but it must be accepted that it will take time. Before the child can ignore distractions he or she needs to be able to identify key elements before blocking them out and providing alternative filtering strategies so that distractions lose their attraction.

One way to start this process is for a child to make a list of which distractions attract them the most in every class. With younger children this may require help from an adult, but once this has been done it may help to pinpoint physical distractions that could be removed or at least adapted to some extent. It may also be possible to help identify whether visual or auditory distractions are most common. The next thing is to record the strength of the distractions and the time they took from the main objective.

One method of beating distractions is the distraction zapper. This is a method of turning unwanted distractions into a game in which children record successful attempts to ignore distractions that would otherwise lead away from their priority tasks. The zapper could be constructed as an imaginary laser gun for children to zap the distractions. They could even perhaps record how many hits they get, as they might in a laser quest game.

Teaching this by role-play with supervisor and child can yield the best results but, as always, trial and error will play a part. Don't expect perfection – it will never or seldom happen!

Rewards

It is likely, however, that whatever rules are created and however successfully they are introduced they will still often be broken: children with ADHD do not appear to anticipate the consequences of their behaviour nor do they necessarily learn from experience of negative consequences.

Students with ADHD are more likely to comply or be hooked into task completion and behavioural targets if they get something for doing this than if something is taken away for not doing it. This is not to say that sanctions cannot and do not work, and certainly they should always be an option, but it is just that rewards work more effectively if they are used in a positive way. This is probably due to the fact that ADHD students live for the moment, and the idea of a sanction, which usually involves something of a time lag, is less stimulating than a more immediate reward. Children with ADHD consequently need to be rewarded almost immediately.

Let's look at some rewards:

♦ positive comments

♦ stamps, stickers, merits, points, certificates

♦ additional responsibilities in the class

♦ taking classes outside

♦ free time

♦ ICT options

♦ informing parents of positive issues

♦ options involving special areas of interest, e.g. music, art, sports

♦ freedom of movement

♦ choice of work/class options

♦ field trips, outings

♦ lunch with head teacher (yes, some kids *do* like this)

♦ reduced homework

♦ phone tokens, food, money (for older students).

Overall, although the range of rewards listed above is extensive, some may appear extravagant, for example the possible use of money for older students. However, the principle element is that in most cases everybody has a price. The key is establishing what that price is.

For younger students, feeding the fish or cleaning out the hamster cage is a major reward, but for a more angry and sullen 15-year-old the options will be rather different. Of course I am not suggesting that schools or teachers 'pay students' to work or behave, but if recognition of performance is recorded and passed on to parents and carers, and this works for the child, then it is an option worth looking at.

Similarly, food might also be considered. I am not suggesting anyone should starve or be given lots of sweets, cakes and chocolate but if food is an incentive for some students then their position in the lunch queue might be an important factor for them.

Rewards should only ever be given consistently and in a businesslike way as recognition of compliance and/or task completion. The response must be kept immediate, as long-term recognition of the child's achievement will be lost in cyberspace.

What works for one student, however, might not work for another; and what works one day might not work the next. Finding reward systems that work consistently is a constantly dynamic process.

Sanctions

The key element of using sanctions is to try to keep the sanction as private as possible. In some cases, it is not possible to do this and then you should appear 'to regret the action you have been forced to take'. In addition, it is always useful to reaffirm the point that it is the actions of the pupil that are being dealt with and not the pupil themselves. Depersonalizing the situation is very important for all students, but especially for students with ADHD.

The other main point with applying sanctions is that the student will always feel that he or she has a choice of either complying or not complying and that the decision is theirs. Step-by-step sanctions can be applied, gradually building up if a student fails to comply with the initial request made by a teacher who (even if angry and frustrated) must remain professional and appear cool on the outside. Finally, it may be useful to offer a 'suspended sanction', i.e. one that could be deactivated if the student complies for the remainder of a set period as determined by the teacher.

Some options in the sanctions list could be:

♦ displeasure of supervisor

♦ docking points, merits, etc.

♦ choice of teacher where to seat student

♦ restriction of free time at break/lunch

♦ time out

♦ informing parents of negative issues

♦ detention

♦ removal of privileges

♦ fines

♦ removal from a specific class for a fixed period

♦ removal from school for a fixed period.

As with rewards, the key with sanctions is to apply them consistently in a businesslike way. The emphasis must be on a proactive rather than a reactive response. The child needs to register his or her mistake so that he or she will not do it again.

It is important that the sanction is given as clearly and quickly as possible. It should be delivered, if at all possible, away from the group. Public floggings seldom pay dividends.

Having said this, what works well for some students works less successfully for others. Some students respond better to a sanction-loaded framework than to rewards. It is not possible to follow a 'one size fits all' approach.

Controlling Aggression

One area that I think we need to be clear about, however, concerns aggression – either physical or verbal – towards peers or teachers. Despite the fact that the aggression may stem from the frustration of difficulty in learning or other experiences, and not all children who exhibit aggression have long-standing problems, aggression warrants our full attention.

Reversing aggression can take a great deal of time and supervision and in some cases the issues are multi-faceted in origin and therefore need to be managed in a multi-agency way. However, the same principles need to be applied in most, if not all, cases.

'Aggression towards others will result in logical consequences.' There is no other option for students who regularly exhibit this trait: they need to be trained that their behaviour will result in an immediate negative response with no warning necessary. Further to this, the two techniques of overcorrection and positive practice should be utilized. For example, when a student gets so mad that he picks up a chair and throws it against the wall, breaking the chair in the process, the following should take place.

1. The student goes to the time out area until in control.

2. The student pays for the replacement of the chair.

3. The student tidies all the chairs under the desks in that class at the end of the day for the next two weeks.

I am sure some of you reading this will be sceptical about whether this process would ever actually happen. However, the principle is that if it doesn't it is likely that real change will never occur. Even then it is likely that other incidents will need a similar approach. 'Who has the time?' I hear you say. Well, 'make the time' is the only answer I can give you. Time spent on this will save you a lot more time and resources in the long run.

Other ways of dealing with aggression include teaching the child to use hesitation and calming techniques before the red mist descends, and finding alternative ways of dealing with aggressive feelings and attitudes. Some or all of the following should be involved in this approach: counsellors; peer mentors; form tutors; parents; social services; health professionals.

Working with the ADHD Diagnosis in Behaviour Management

Although behaviour management may be about the use of specific systems and strategies it is really about how people respond to certain situations. It is also about how individual teachers respond to issues of non-compliance and the poor social skills of students with ADHD.

Teachers will therefore need to look at their own levels of performance, patience and, to some extent, their relationships with pupils in order to decide how successful they are in managing specific individuals who may be demanding, defiant and different.

Some principles for teachers to consider are as follows:

◆ teachers need to consider their own response to the situation

◆ the way in which adult supervisors behave towards any child often influences the way that other children react towards the child

◆ teachers and other professionals themselves need understanding and acceptance from other colleagues

◆ teachers need to consider how to use their power over other students.

The issue of power is all-important, as is how the teacher applies their power to determine an outcome. Olsen and Cooper (2001: 201) outline teacher power in the following way:

1. Coercive power: based on punishment.

2. Record power: praise/appraisal.

3. Legitimate power: status of teacher or student.

4. Referral power: liking/respect of teacher/pupil.

5. Expert power: respect of knowledge.

These five bases of power are divided into two groups: 1, 2 and 3 are positional powers; 4 and 5 are personal powers.

All teachers have their own style of managing their classrooms and individual students based on their own personalities and their interpretation of how the rules should be adhered to and applied.

As I mentioned before, students with ADHD will be engaged if they are interested or attracted to the person who is managing them, depending on the principles above. It is for each individual teacher to assess how much power they want to exhibit when working with each pupil.

Finally, no chapter on intervention would be complete without some of the 'dos and don'ts' of behaviour management which, while not specific to students with ADHD, are suitable for all. Having said this, due to the fact that ADHD students are often better visual than aural learners, the principle that 65 per cent of redirection of student behaviour should be done non-verbally is certainly applicable.

As a result, although short sharp verbal redirection is effective, non-verbal responses through eye contact, facial expression, hand gestures and even physical proximity to students should be used in place of verbal instructions. It is also always useful to list the issues that in a heated situation would inflame the participants even further; and those that might defuse the situation.

Inflaming:

♦ shouting

♦ bringing up past conflicts

♦ not listening to their views

♦ face to face (toe to toe)

♦ voice raising

♦ finger pointing, teeth baring

♦ allowing conflict in a public forum.

Defusing:

♦ calm but assertive

♦ let them speak

♦ palm of hand/hands by side

♦ time out options/escape hatch

♦ divert attention

♦ offer a choice

♦ use silence

♦ refer to rights and responsibilities

♦ use humour if appropriate.

ADHD

Overall, successful behaviour management of students with ADHD and related issues is about developing a sense of proportion about the situation. If you see incidents as problems then that really is the problem. However, if you view them as opportunities or challenges then they become more interesting and rewarding. It can be frustrating but it can be fun. In short, the best advice I can give is to be firm and fair, be consistent in your actions and 'regret the punishment' when necessary. This should ensure success and keep the grey hairs at bay.

5

Intervention: Socialization Options

Selfish	Low Self esteem
Egocentric	Loud/Quiet
Anxious	Boisterous
Rude	Thoughtless
Insensitive	Withdrawn
Immature	Without Feeling
Depressed	Doesn't take Turns

These are just some of the ways in which students with ADHD are described by peers, siblings and parents.

Pupils with ADHD can initially appear quite amusing to other students, but this 'class clown' effect soon wears thin and is rapidly replaced by impatience and intolerance of the constant interruptions that may often take place. This can subsequently lead to the isolation of the individual concerned from the peer group.

Parents are often more concerned with this issue than with their child's academic standing. They identify it, quite rightly, as a crucial area of their child's development of self-esteem and his or her happiness. They will often have vast experience of the problem. In many cases the child will have been excluded from invitations to other children's birthday parties and other social events from the age of 2 upwards. They may have been regarded as too unruly or too different to attend. Having troubled relations with siblings at home may also compound this situation.

In this chapter we will look at some specific situations in both the school and the home environment and consider options for the future.

It is one of the strange but true ironies that students with ADHD have tremendous problems in relating to people of their own age and seem to get on better with either much younger or older people. It often seems as if they are 'off the pace' and out of step with their chronological age group and they are often better able to communicate with either younger or older students.

This is one of the reasons why the ADHD child may be very articulate in the presence of adults, who cannot understand why on earth he/she should be regarded as having a problem at school. It is with their peers, however, that the problems mainly appear, and in order to compete in the marketplace of friendship sometimes dramatic tactics are needed.

Harry just didn't understand why no one liked him, and boy did he want to be liked! Ryan used to be his friend but now he hung around with Marco's crowd. As for the girls, they just teased him. As a result he decided he would make them take notice. He decided he would start to take things belonging to those students who shunned and ignored him. Of course Harry was not very good at stealing, as successful theft requires planning and patience. Harry didn't consider the details or the consequences. He was impulsive in his choices and reckless in his execution.

> During the parent/teacher conference, after the obligatory period of denial, Harry broke down in tears and admitted the offences. He cried, 'I had to do it, it was the only way of getting their attention.' (adapted from O'Regan 2002)

The relationship between students is both complex and often misunderstood by adults: only the pupils can relate to the specifics of why they fall into and out of friendships. Often, when teachers or parents try to understand why problems occur they will find it difficult to relate to the current context as students may have great difficulty in explaining exactly what the problem is or was.

It can take hours to extract the core problem, which may have started out as some trivial incident but which may have grown into serious confrontation or profound unhappiness between former friends. Students can punch each other's lights out one minute and be 'bosom buddies' the next; they can be at each other's throats during school but spend time together at the weekend and share family trips. It's all in the lap of the gods.

While all teenagers need supportive relationships, adolescents with ADHD are especially in need of guidance from caring adults, especially when faced with academic and social adjustment problems. Teenagers who make it through tough times will need to do so in a supportive context. It appears to be a common factor that whether the support came from a particular teacher, teaching assistant, counsellor or patient and proactive parent the net result is always the same. 'I had someone who cared' or 'someone believed in me' is so often the comment of the successful ADHD college student.

As a result, positive relationships are the cornerstone to the action needed and are at least as important as the specific strategies already outlined. Strong emotional bonds between adults and teens provide the backdrop against which failure and fears can be explored. This is where plans can be made about how to react in different problem situations, where motivation can be nurtured and encouragement given.

Talking to the Rest of the Class about the Student with ADHD

Unlike a child with a physical handicap, whose disability is often visually apparent, students with ADHD or with a mental handicap are not always obvious to other students. As a result they may be subjected to bullying or simply avoided by fellow students, who may feel that they are fair targets or 'freaks'.

Victims of bullying are often 'provocative victims'. This means they provoke other students to gain attention. Then there are the students who become bullies themselves in order to achieve recognition amongst their classmates. This may well be another avenue for attention-seeking individuals.

In order to explain to other students why certain students behave differently a number of different techniques can be used in schools, including:

♦ circle time

♦ advanced circle time

♦ personal, social and health education (PSHE)

♦ citizenship classes

♦ role-play/drama options.

The degree of success or failure of some or all of these programmes will vary from child to child. The expectations and culture of individual schools will also be a big influence, along with the skills of the staff in providing inclusive education, and the support of families.

Other effective resources are materials that explain or sell the fact that children with ADHD are not usually annoying, disruptive or jerks. A particularly good programme of materials is produced by Michael Gordon, which includes a series of books for siblings of children with ADHD. *My Brother is a World Class Pain* is particularly useful.

Many problems for children with ADHD stem from their inability to handle the various degrees of environmental stimuli that come their way. This is why they operate best within a consistent structure that provides them with safety and security. It tells them precisely what they need to do to stay on task and out of trouble.

As a result, any change in the structure or routine of the standard school day needs to be carefully considered and planned for the child with ADHD, as changes may undermine the systems employed and present a whole new set of variables, which may cause problems for the child and their supervisors.

Therefore, careful consideration must be given to all non-classroom time such as break/lunchtime and during sports/other activities where socialization problems between students can and will occur. It is to be recommended that break and lunchtime periods be structured as much as possible for students with ADHD. Effective personnel should supervise and set up programmes during these times.

It is a myth that children with ADHD will 'burn off' excess energy at break if they are allowed to do what they want. In reality these students return to class pumped up and are then even more difficult to settle. In addition, unsupervised team games such as football and basketball are not usually a good idea because ADHD students may find themselves excluded and possibly even victimized by less tolerant individuals.

As many of these students may have co-existing fine and gross motor coordination difficulties, certain activities are best avoided. Individual activities or sports are often a better option. One team game that can be tried, however, is football, but beware of the consequences when working with specific students!

Justin was actually rather a good basketball player who could leap like a gazelle and had excellent hand–eye coordination. Once employed in the football goalkeeping position, he appeared in practice sessions to be an excellent shot saver and due to his hyperactive/impulsive ADHD was able to dominate his penalty area (a crucial characteristic for a goalkeeper). In fact, he became so adept at plucking opposing team crosses from out of the air it was not long before he became known as 'the Cat'.

When the day came, our assembled team prepared themselves for the honour of representing the school against the neighbouring comprehensive. It was to be a 'David versus Goliath' affair. Despite the odds we started brightly and went one goal up due to a move we called 'the rush'. This was in fact a tactic we had no control over. Despite hours of training to the contrary, whenever Justin received the ball his impulsive nature ensured that he booted it up the field as if it were a live grenade. This would occur whether his own players were ready or not.

It was on one of these many occasions that the opposition, not being used to such a fast game plan, had been caught napping and our inside right profited from Justin's swift clearance to score with some panache.

As the game progressed during the first half it was end-to-end stuff, quite literally, as Justin was saving everything thrown at him. He belted the ball in a frenzy into the opposing half as soon as he collected it, even though we had no players in the vicinity.

At half time, although we were 2–1 down we were not disheartened as we were playing quite well and had the wind in our favour for the second half.

As the game restarted, despite some early scares, when the wind propelled Justin's clearances, we encamped in the opposing half and scored twice more to take a 3–2 lead.

One other major factor that helped our cause was the fear the opposing school had of Chloe Shaw who, due to our limited playing resources, was one of two girls we had drafted into the team. She was playing in an area we can loosely refer to as 'midfield' but as far as she was concerned this actually covered a zone of five square metres, beyond which she never ventured. Chloe had inattentive ADHD and wasn't very well coordinated. With her flowing blonde locks she didn't look like much of a threat. She appeared uninterested as she stood, hands on hips, oblivious to all around her. She was in her own dream world staring into the distance, until she was shaken from her trance by someone yelling 'Chloe, ball!'

Upon this command, Chloe exploded into action, hurtling towards the ball, or, more accurately, to where it had been the previous time she had looked. Unfortunately for the opposition, Chloe did not discriminate and, travelling at great speed, annihilated at least four different players on separate occasions after the ball had long gone elsewhere. These players climbed gingerly to their feet, shook their heads and vowed in future to take seriously the impending threat to their lives Chloe presented. Chloe, meanwhile, would drift back into what appeared a semi-comatose dreamlike state after each tackle until the next time a command was issued.

With time running out we pressurized the opposition and a fourth goal looked likely. But we suddenly lost possession, which resulted in the opposing centre forward sprinting into our half of the field and bearing down on our goal.

All my thoughts told me that this was a job for the Cat; he would save the game for us. However, on closer inspection, Justin was not in his goal. In fact he was nowhere near it, but could be seen in the distance on a bicycle in the playground area adjacent to the field.

The centre forward shot into an empty net to tie the game. He turned to his team-mates to celebrate.

Meanwhile, the rest of the team were most unhappy with Cat, apart from Chloe, who said 'Ah, bless him.'

(Adapted from stories in O'Regan (2002), and Cooper and O'Regan (2001))

As this football game clearly shows, children with ADHD can be engaged in sports events as long as they are actively participating. Any period of non-involvement, however, will result in them finding something else to do or getting into mental drift. For this reason certain sports with prolonged periods of inactivity, such as fielding in cricket or softball, are to be avoided.

Communication Between School and Parents

There is an old African saying that 'it takes a village to raise a child'. This is most definitely true in the case of students with ADHD.

Effective and proactive relationships between parents and schools is vital to the overall success of dealing with students with ADHD. The impact on the families of children with ADHD is often immeasurable. That is in stark contrast to school life where, although teachers may feel an individual student takes up all their time, the actual amount of time that a pupil spends within the school is only about 15 to 18 per cent of an average school year. This means that roughly 80 per cent of the time the child is under the parent's jurisdiction. This is a full-time job for those involved.

Generally parents try to act in the best interests of

their child at all times. Their actions are usually based on the information available to them at the time. If there appears to be a contradiction between what the so-called 'professionals' advise and what the parents act on, then there is usually a good reason for this. Parents have to find their own way of both accepting and dealing with a problem in the light of their own circumstances.

It is not uncommon, however, for parents of ADHD children to experience conflict with each other. For example, the father might blame the mother for not keeping the child under control. The mother might explain that nothing she does seems to work. Fathers, despite their potential for helping the situation, can sometimes react in an unhelpful way, such as avoiding going home until the child is asleep or taking sides with the child against the mother.

Some ways of helping parents are to try to get them to put into perspective issues that, although annoying, are not life-threatening, and to encourage them to be proactive rather than reactive. The third and most important piece of advice is to have the patience of a saint and/or invest in a golden retriever or Labrador.

The option of a pet, if possible a dog with a good temperament, is an extremely good idea, especially for older children. Dogs offer unconditional love and do not judge children in the same way as peers, siblings or parents. At the end of a difficult day, when everyone in the world seems to have screamed at the child, a Rover or Lola will do the job of being a friend. One major disadvantage, however, is that you can't assume that the ADHD child will look after all the needs of their pet.

Parents may sometimes try to transfer the problems they are experiencing at home to individual teachers at school. While it is valuable and correct for teachers and parents to work together towards academic goals, it is important that teachers do not get dragged into domestic issues for which they are neither trained nor have the energy or time to support. The key element in working with parents is communication. As long as this is taking place during both the good times and the not so good, no surprises will occur. In most cases this will ensure that parents will work alongside the school in managing the child with ADHD.

Frequent telephone/text contact, frequent parent–teacher conferences and possibly daily report cards can all be vehicles to help prevent misunderstandings occurring between the parents and school. Good communication will also ensure that any possible manipulation of the situation by a specific child can be headed off by close and proactive contact. In certain cases, such as severe anger management issues, serious socialization issues where breakdown or major friction between students and parents and teachers have occurred, counselling, mentoring and/or coaching may be required.

Two considerations that must be remembered at all times are that:

♦ children with ADHD can place a great deal of pressure on family relationships, especially if they also have ODD

♦ in persistently difficult situations the possibility of unrecognized parental ADHD and ODD should be considered.

71

ADHD

There are many excellent programmes designed to help parents come to terms with problems between each other, in their relationship with the child and with other members of the family. Home management techniques can be taught through role-play and, to some extent, group therapy. The success of these programmes depends largely on the quality of counsellor and the openness of all parties to objective advice.

The best quality that a counsellor can have is to be 'uncluttered and uncomplicated'. They also need to focus on one or two specific issues and develop strategies to help parents 'help themselves' in the future. There is a fine line between helping the child come to terms with their problems and adapting or learning the rules of socialization. It is important that the child isn't thrown even further into a pit of despair from which there is no way out.

Although a wide variety of issues are dealt with on a daily basis, one of the core features that ADHD children suffer from is anger. This anger can be directed at many sources – parents, siblings, teachers, and peers are all in the firing line.

The role of the counsellor can often be very lonely as much of the information received is, by its very nature, confidential and cannot be easily shared, especially when dealing with delicate family issues. In many cases parents themselves will need a great deal of support. Some of the essential elements of parental training are:

♦ family education about ADHD

♦ maximizing the impact of medication

♦ problem-solving skills

♦ communication skills

♦ restoring parental control

♦ reframing/restructuring

♦ tension reduction

♦ individual psychotherapy where indicated.

There is no doubt that working with children with ADHD can leave its mark on you, which is illustrated in the following anecdote.

One lunchtime I returned to the school gate with a tuna sandwich from the Londis across the road, my keys and two one pound coins. I was confused as to why I was carrying the coins until I realized to my horror that – while my mind was in such a spin about many different issues – I must have gone into the shop, picked up the sandwich and then left without paying.

Returning to the shop and looking suitably embarrassed, I apologized to the shopkeeper for my forgetfulness. I was about to give him the two pound coins for the £1.60 sandwich when he said that actually I owed him £3.20 as this would include the one I hadn't paid for yesterday.

There is now a sign on the door which says 'only two teachers allowed in at a time'.

6

Intervention: Multi-agency Options

One question often asked these days is why ADHD has suddenly become such a buzzword when so many other terms related to behaviour already exist within the SEN framework. Where has it come from and how did it first appear on the horizon?

The answer, of course, is that it is not a new term. The symptoms were within the realms of the 1990 International Criteria of Diseases (ICD10) and described as 'Hyperkinetic Disorder'. This category basically classifies only children who have both the combined AD/HD criteria of hyperactive/impulsive and inattentive symptoms. Using these criteria only 0.5 per cent of children would be regarded as having hyperkinetic disorder, in contrast with the three to eight per cent of the student population who are diagnosed with the broader AD/HD term in the USA (S. Goldstein and M. Goldstein, 1992).

The question is, where does ADHD fit within the current SEN and behaviour platform? One policy that has altered the perception of ADHD is the 2003 Disability and Discrimination Act, which complements the Revised Code of Practice (2001). It provides clear guidance that ADHD is indeed a disability and as such must be catered for both in the workplace and the broader community.

As with most disabilities, the management of ADHD is often multi-disciplinary; a number of agencies may need to be involved alongside the school, including health and social services, housing and youth offending teams.

On the issue of youth offending there have been a number of recent multi-agency contracts designed to include antisocial behaviour contracts (ABCs). These are written agreements between a young person, the local housing office or landlord and the local police. The contracts outline behaviour targets for persistent offenders and are aimed at young persons aged 10 to 18.

These contracts, along with parenting contracts (PCs) and Anti-Social Behavioural Orders (ASBOs) are a prime example of the current focus on multi-agency cooperation. Although, of course, most children with ADHD are not responsible for youth offending, if the condition is not dealt with the risk factors for offending can increase. It is hoped that the framework encouraged by the recent Green Paper, Every Child Matters (September 2003), and the new paper on SEN, Raising Barriers to Achievement (2004) as well as the new Children's Bill (2004) will start to function for the children who at present have fallen through the cracks or who are caught up in the system.

Recent Research

A recent research report (*ADHD: Paying enough attention*) conducted across health professionals in the UK in 2003 found the following key issues:

1. There are a number of barriers to diagnosis and treatment.

2. ADHD is underdiagnosed.

3. Underdiagnosed and untreated ADHD has a significant impact on a person's life.

In addition, the survey included the following findings:

♦ 54 per cent of UK health professionals stated that ADHD is underdiagnosed in the UK

♦ 43 per cent of specialists said that teachers were not aware of ADHD so they didn't realize children should be referred

♦ 54 per cent of specialists felt GPs were unsure of which parents to refer

♦ 90 per cent felt ADHD can lead to difficulties in finding a job and keeping a job

♦ 97 per cent stated that children with underdiagnosed ADHD are more likely to drop out of school several years earlier than their peers

♦ 85 per cent said that not treating childhood ADHD can lead to adult mental health problems such as depression and even suicide

♦ 98 per cent of specialists stated that behavioural therapy together with pharmacotherapy is the most effective way of treating ADHD, yet only 34 per cent use this for their patients.

Their key recommendations for the future included the following.

ADHD

1. Teachers need increased education and resources to support them in the classroom and to help provide advice to parents about how to access the healthcare system.

2. GPs should receive further information about ADHD in order to improve levels of appropriate referral for secondary care and diagnosis to ensure they can provide the ongoing observation and support needed if the diagnosis is made.

3. Secondary care needs additional specialists to ensure that the waiting time is shortened for a first referral and that they can see patients more often.

4. Patients should have access to the most effective management strategy, which currently does not happen due to parental concerns regarding medication.

5. There needs to be a greater understanding of ADHD amongst the general public and the media in order to remove the fear of being branded or blamed as a failure.

6. There needs to be more information to help parents increase their understanding and ensure they seek help from their GP.

One of the central issues facing both Local Education Authorities (LEAs) and health professionals is the cost of provision if large numbers of students are diagnosed with the condition and only a few schools (and staff) are experienced or trained to deliver an appropriate multi-modal management approach, especially if one of the options includes the use of medication.

Medication

The use of medication to manage the condition remains the key issue in national acceptance and understanding of this issue. Though not always necessary or appropriate in a number of cases, medication is one option for managing the condition. However, this is an area that clearly divides public opinion and hinders the recognition of ADHD.

Many alternatives to medication exist, not least a number of highly effective and successful dietary and nutritional adaptations. These include:

♦ long-chain polysaturates such as efflex and other oils

♦ fatty acid supplements

♦ zinc sulphate

♦ other mineral supplements.

Other options include eliminating monosodium glutamate (MSG), various additives and high-sugar products from the child's diet. Many of the advocates of this approach claim 'we are what we eat', and research would seem to show that diet is a factor. However, medication remains the single most effective treatment for children and adolescents with severe hyperactivity and impulsivity.

To some extent this is not surprising: if ADHD is a neurobiochemical condition caused by lack of specific neurotransmitters, then it is likely that in many cases a neurobiochemical solution is needed. As it is thought that neurotransmitters are responsible for relaying information between various parts of the brain necessary for certain functions to take place (e.g. impulse control and concentration), dysregulation in this complex chemical relay system appears to cause emotional and behavioural problems. As stated by Cooper in 1995, 'medication is employed not as a chemical cosh to sedate overactive or inattentive children but as a chemical facilitator that raises chronically low levels of activity in certain parts of the brain and so regulates the message-carrying process.'

Currently the neuro-stimulants methylphenidate (Ritalin) and dexamphetaphine (Dexedrine) are the most commonly used and effective preparations for treating ADHD. Dosage levels vary from individual to individual but the general rule of thumb is 1.5mg per kg of body weight for Ritalin and 0.75mg per kg of body weight for Dexedrine over a four-hour activation period. However, other non-stimulant options, namely Atomoxetine HCl (Strattera), are also now available in the UK and provide an alternative to traditional medication treatment options.

Not all children enjoy taking medication, however, even though it may be helping them academically, behaviourally and socially. Some students do not like to feel different and can also be embarrassed by taking medication as they might be teased by their peers. In addition, a minority of students may suffer from minor side effects such as stomach upsets, especially in the early stages.

The best way of handling these issues is for the child to meet the supervising paediatrician or psychologist, who can then explain why the medication is being used. As always, a judgement of benefits against costs needs to be made. Any side effects can usually be eradicated by making minor changes to the dosage or the time at which the pills are administered.

One crucial aspect to bear in mind is that for any child on medication, it is the parents who are in charge rather than the doctors, physiologists or teachers. Although the decision as to whether or not medication is prescribed lies with the physician, parents are fully entitled to choose whether they follow the professional's prescription or reject it.

Here is a brief overview of some of the issues associated with using medication.

When Should Medication be Used?

♦ Only after comprehensive evaluation.

♦ When a child is at significant risk of harming him/herself or others.

♦ When serious attempts at non-medical interventions have proved insufficient.

♦ When the child is at risk of emotional and/or academic failure.

Medication for ADHD

A 12-step process regarding medication use could be:

1. Comprehensive diagnosis of ADHD.

2. Remediation tried.

3. Counselling provided.

4. Structured learning environment offered.

5. Observation of progress.

6. If no progress made consider whether medication is necessary.

7. Base rate of medication established.

8. Trial period on medication.

9. Adjustments where necessary.

10. Benefits/disadvantages analysed.

11. Continuation determined on step 10.

12. Possible medication breaks – annually, during school holidays or after set period.

Overview

These are the key components in the area of medication policy, provision and practice.

♦ The use of medication alone in the treatment of ADHD is not recommended. As indicated earlier, a multi-modal treatment plan is usually followed for successful treatment of the ADHD child or adolescent.

♦ While not all children with ADHD are prescribed medication, in certain cases the proper use of medication can play an important and necessary part in the child's overall treatment.

♦ Ritalin, the most commonly used medication for treating ADHD, is a psycho-stimulant and has been prescribed for many years with very favourable results and minimal side-effects.

◆ Other psycho-stimulant medications used to treat ADHD are Dexedrine, Equasym and Concerta. Some antidepressant medications such as Imipramine, non-stimulants such as Atomoxetine (Strattera) and tranquilizer drugs such as Risperidone have also proved successful in treating the disorder. All these medications are believed to affect the body's neurotransmitter chemicals, deficiencies of which may be the cause of ADHD. In addition, the anti-hypertensive drug Clonidine, which treats high blood pressure, has also been used for treating ADHD.

◆ Improvements in such characteristics as attention span, impulse control and hyperactivity are noted in approximately 75 per cent of children who take psycho-stimulant medications.

◆ It is important that teachers are informed about all the medications that an ADHD student may take, as they need to work closely with the child's parents and other helping professionals in monitoring medication effectiveness.

◆ Side effects such as appetite loss, sleeping difficulties and/or lethargy in the classroom can often be controlled through medication dosage adjustments.

What Parents Need to Know About Medication

There is a lot of misinformation regarding the use of medication in the treatment of ADHD. These are the facts that every parent needs to know:

- although stimulant medication needs to be handled wisely, it can be administered safely and effectively

- stimulants do not turn children into zombies, axe murderers or dwarfs

- stimulants are non-addictive and don't produce a 'high'

- any signs of tics, withdrawal, odd behaviour or poor health should be reported immediately even if you are unsure about the problem or worried about being wrong

- medication should be considered in a child with significant ADHD

- there is currently significant under-medication in the UK

- parents and professionals must be factually advised of the rationale for using medication as well as possible side effects

- fine-tuning of dosage, both in quality and timing, is essential for effective management

- combinations of medications are sometimes necessary in complex cases. (adapted from Kewley 1999)

Parent Support Groups

Despite all the challenges and problems of dealing with children with ADHD, the future in terms of both recognition and provision is looking extremely bright. This is largely due to the growth of parent support groups.

In much the same way that dyslexia awareness

parent support groups forced both the education system and employers to take notice of this issue 40 years ago the same battle is currently being fought by parents (though in many cases more accurately mothers) of children with ADHD.

A recent two-day consultation conference in Southport organized by the ADHD parent support group ADDISS brought parents together from all over the UK, all of whom were concerned about ADHD. An initial questionnaire given to parents to find out more about their experiences found that while some parents said diagnosis took less than six months, almost a quarter reported that this process took between one and five years, thereby placing those children at an extreme disadvantage. Other key findings were:

♦ three-quarters of children with ADHD receive medication

♦ for one in six children medication started before the age of six

♦ a diagnosis is usually made by a consultant in psychiatry, psychology or paediatrics

♦ very few consultants offer a support group, let alone provide details of other support groups

♦ more than half of the parents reported that a support group had been the most valuable resource for them

♦ time and time again social services were deemed the most unhelpful group. Most parents said social services didn't recognize ADHD as a disability and rarely offered support for respite care

- all parents agreed that training was vital. However, only a tiny minority found that teachers in their child's school received specific training in ADHD
- 50 per cent of children with ADHD have a Statement of Special Educational Needs
- experience of positive change is largely dependent on individual professionals rather than through a managed organizational approach
- one in four affected children had been apprehended for anti-social behaviour or another youth offence.

Parents were also asked to say what had made the most difference to them and their family. The vast majority said 'Getting a diagnosis and treatment'. But for one family, 'The single biggest difference is Mr Matthew Brown, Year 3 teacher at Whitton Green Primary School, Lowestoft, Suffolk', which just goes to show how different children need different solutions.

In summary, parents felt that the following would make the biggest difference to their children and families:

1. Training for all professionals concerned.

2. Improved communication between parents, schools, health services and social care.

3. Early intervention to get diagnosis and treatment as soon as possible.

4. Raised awareness of the condition, the issues and the positives.

5. Consistency of services and policies locally and nationally.

6. More information for parents and children.

7. Resourcing the right things in the right place.

The Future of ADHD

An all-party parliamentary group, chaired by Kerry Pollard MP, recently met to discuss ADHD. Their focus was the following:

◆ to raise awareness and understanding amongst parliamentarians of the nature of the condition and its impact on sufferers, families and society as a whole

◆ to crystallize the activities that many MPs are engaged in at constituency level and to harness these energies and provide cross-party drivers of change

◆ to encourage a joined-up response from relevant government departments that will address the needs of ADHD suffers and their families (DfES, Home Office, DoH, DWP and DEFRA)

◆ in short, an understanding of ADHD and its related problems is critical in managing the behaviour and securing the happiness of many young people in both our schools and society.

Summary

ADHD is not an excuse for disruptive or inappropriate behaviour but rather an explanation for why specific individuals may act in a way that other people find annoying and unacceptable. An understanding of the ADHD condition creates a range of possibilities for effective treatment and management, in the same way that a child who has dyslexia is not lazy or stupid but requires a different adaptive approach to access the written or spoken word.

In many ways ADHD is undergoing a similar pattern to the recognition of dyslexia in the UK, where the pioneers who fought for the rights of dyslexic children were initially accused of creating a 'middle-class syndrome' to excuse poor academic performance. Parents of dyslexic children, with commitment, passion and belief in their cause, coaxed, lobbied and fought for the rights of their children to be properly understood by teachers and the government. As a result they have achieved national and international recognition of dyslexia and have generated holistic provision, acceptance and funding for many of those affected.

Parent power once again will be the main agent for change in policy, process and provision for children with ADHD.

It is an unfortunate fact that many children with ADHD within the school community are likely to be experiencing an unsuccessful and unhappy time. In many cases these children are even excluded from the school community. This is a complete tragedy that in so many cases could, should and would be avoided by understanding the impact and applying proactive management interventions to help these children help themselves.

No one ever said, however, that managing children

is easy, as this cutting taken from a teacher's notice-board in a local primary school states quite clearly:

After creating Heaven and Earth, God created Adam and Eve, and the first thing he said was 'DON'T'.

'Don't what?' asked Adam.

'Don't eat the forbidden fruit,' God said.

'Forbidden fruit? We have forbidden fruit? Hey, Eve, we have forbidden fruit!!!'

'No way.'

'Yes way.'

'Do *not* eat the fruit,' said God.

'Why?'

'Because I am your father and I said so,' God replied, wondering why he hadn't stopped after creating elephants. A few minutes later God saw his children having an apple break and he was miffed.

'Didn't I tell you not to eat the fruit?' God asked.

'Uh huh,' Adam replied.

'Then why did you do it?'

'I don't know,' said Eve.

'She started it,' said Adam.

'Did not.'

'Did too.'

'DID NOT!"

In order for them to understand the importance of rules, God's decision was that Adam and Eve should have children of their own, and thus was set a pattern that has never changed.

The moral of this story is that if you have persistently tried to consistently manage children, do not be too hard on yourself. If God had problems raising children, what makes you think it would be a piece of cake for you?

Appendix 1

Specific Learning Difficulties

Dyslexia

Also known as SpLD (specific learning difficulty), dyslexia is a condition that presents itself in all ranges of ability and often leads to persistent difficulty in acquiring literacy. Associated problems can include sequencing, organization, fine motor control and directional difficulties. There is often a familial link and the degree of difficulty can vary greatly between individuals. Said to affect approximately ten to 20 per cent of the population, it exists throughout the intellectual range. It generally affects boys more than girls, but tends to run in families. That there is a strong genetic element was recently backed up by the mapping of pieces of chromosomal material that might possibly be responsible. Many people with dyslexia also have problems with the sounds that make up words, as well as difficulties in word interpretation, perception, sequencing, writing and spelling. On the plus side, many dyslexics have strong creative talents in the arts, design, computing and lateral thinking.

Dyscalculia

This is essentially concerned with deficits in the learning of mathematics. This may include difficulties in understanding and recalling the concept of number and number relationships, and difficulties in learning and applying comprehension of word problems. Recent estimates suggest that between three and six per cent of the population is affected by dyscalculia. Dyscalculia may be developmental, in which case the student has always experienced difficulties in the subject, or it may be acquired, in that the student's arithmetic ability was formerly at a higher level. Developmental dyscalculia is considered to be a disorder of the abilities to deal with numbers and calculating developed at an early age and is not accompanied by coexisting disabilities.

Dyspraxia (DCD)

This is associated with an inability to organize movement. Dyspraxics can often display problems with language, both spoken and written. The cause of dyspraxia is thought to be related to immature neuronal development and many individuals improve levels of competence as they mature. Approximately one child in 20 suffers from the condition, with boys affected four times more frequently than girls.

Characteristics to look out for include:

◆ difficulties with fine or gross motor skills

◆ sensitivity to touch

◆ poor short-term memory

◆ cannot answer simple questions even if they know the answer

Appendix 1: Specific Learning Difficulties

♦ speech problems, slowness in learning to speak or incoherent speech

♦ engages in immature behaviour and may display temper tantrums

♦ performs better on a one-one basis.

Appendix 2

Autism/Asperger's Syndrome

Autism is a complex disorder and the needs of children in this group can differ greatly, ranging from mild to severe. Children with autism generally have three main areas of difficulty:

◆ **Communication**. Language impairment across all modes of communication: speech, intonation, gesture, facial expression and other body language.

◆ **Imagination**. Rigidity and inflexibility of thought process: resistance to change, obsessional and ritualistic behaviour.

◆ **Socialization**. Difficulties with social relationships, poor social timing, lack of empathy, rejection of normal body contact, inappropriate eye contact.

Asperger's syndrome is often called a higher form of autism. Although this is a little misleading, it essentially means that people with Asperger's may be better able to identify aspects of the world in which we all live. Asperger individuals tend to be of average intelligence and often have better communication skills than autistic children.

Some common features are:

Appendix 2: Autism/Asperger's Syndrome

- literal thinking
- obsession with certain topics that leads to exceptional knowledge in one area
- talking at or lecturing another child rather than engaging in a two-way conversation
- excellent memory
- difficulties with social interaction
- monotonous speech tone
- poor motor coordination
- difficulty in understanding and appreciating other people's feelings and perspectives
- difficulties in reading social cues
- little empathy for others.

Appendix 3

Diagnostic Criteria for Conduct Disorder

A. A repetitive and persistent pattern of behaviour in which the basic rights of others or major age-appropriate societal norms or rules are violated, as manifested by the presence of three (or more) of the following criteria in the past 12 months, with at least one criterion present in the last six months:

Aggression to people and animals

1. Often bullies, threatens or intimidates others.

2. Often initiates physical fights.

3. Had used a weapon that can cause serious physical harm to others (e.g. a bat, brick, broken bottle, knife, gun).

4. Has been physically cruel to people.

5. Has been physically cruel to animals.

6. Has stolen while confronting a victim (e.g. mugging, purse snatching, extortion, armed robbery).

7. Has forced someone into sexual activity.

Appendix 3: Criteria for Conduct Disorder

Destruction of property

8. Has deliberately engaged in fire setting with the intention of causing serious damage.

9. Has deliberately destroyed others' property (other than by fire setting).

Deceitfulness or theft

10. Has broken into someone else's house, building or car.

11. Often lies to obtain goods or favours or to avoid obligations (i.e. cons others).

12. Has stolen items of non-trivial value without confronting a victim (e.g. shoplifting, but without breaking and entering, forgery).

Serious violations of rules

13. Often stays out at night despite parental prohibitions, before the age of 13 years.

14. Has run away from home overnight at least twice while living in parental or parental surrogate home (or once without returning for a lengthy period).

15. Is often truant from school, beginning before the age of 13 years.

B. The disturbance in behaviour causes clinically significant impairment of social, academic or occupational functioning.

C. If the individual is aged 18 years or over, criteria are not met for Antisocial Personality Disorder.

Specify type based on age at onset:

♦ **Childhood-Onset Type**: onset of at least one criterion characteristic of Conduct Disorder prior to 10 years.

♦ **Adolescent-Onset Type**: absence of any criterion characteristic of Conduct Disorder prior to age of 10 years

Specify severity:

♦ **Mild**: few, if any, conduct problems in excess of those required to make the diagnosis and conduct problems causing only minor harm to others.

♦ **Moderate**: number of conduct problems and effect on others intermediate between 'mild' and 'severe'.

♦ **Severe**: many conduct problems in excess of those required to make the diagnosis or conduct problems causing considerable harm to others.

Appendix 4

Diagnostic Criteria for Oppositional Defiant Disorder

A. A pattern of negativistic, hostile and defiant behaviour lasting at least six months, during which four or more of the following are present:

1. Often loses temper.

2. Often argues with adults.

3. Often actively defies or refuses to comply with adults' requests or rules.

4. Often deliberately annoys people.

5. Often blames others for his or her mistakes or behaviour.

6. Is often touchy or easily annoyed by others.

7. Is often angry or resentful.

8. Is often spiteful and vindictive.

Note: consider a criterion met only if the behaviour occurs more frequently than is typically observed in individuals of comparable age and developmental level.
A. The disturbance in behaviour causes clinically significant impairment in social, academic or occupational functioning.

B. The behaviours do not occur exclusively during the course of a psychotic or mood disorder.
C. Criteria are not met for conduct disorder, and, if the individual is aged 18 years or older, criteria are not met for antisocial personality disorder.

References

Barkley, R. (1997) *ADHD and the Nature of Self Control*,
   Cleveland OH: Therapeutic Resources Company
Cooper, P. and O'Regan, F. (2001) *Educating children
   with ADHD*, Routledge Falmer Press
Olsen, J. and Cooper, P. (2001) *Dealing with Disruptive
   Behaviour*, Kogan Page
O'Regan, F. (2002) *How to teach and manage children
   with ADHD*: LDA a division of McGraw-Hill
Gordon, M. (1991) *ADHD/Hyperactivity; A Consumers
   Guide*, New York: GSI Publications
Kewley, G. (1999) *Recognition, Reality and Resolution*,
   LAC Press
Train, A. (1995) *The Bullying Problem*, Souvenir Press
Warber, S., Daniels-Garber, M. and Freedman Spizman
   R. (1995) *Helping the ADD/Hyperactive Child*, Villard
   Books

Further Resources

Cooper, P. and O'Regan, F. (2001) *Educating Children with ADHD*, Routledge Falmer Press

Cowley, S. (2003) *Getting the Buggers to Behave 2*, Continuum

Hornsby, B. (1996), *Overcoming Dyslexia: A guide for families and teachers*, Vermilion

Jordan, Rita and Powell, Stuart (1995), *Understanding and Teaching Children with Autism*, John Wiley and Sons

Long, Rob (2000), *Making Sense of Behaviour*, NASEN

Martin, Deirdre (2000), *Teaching Children with Speech and Language Difficulties*, David Fulton

Neanon, Chris, *Active Literacy Kit*, LDA, a division of McGraw-Hill

Neanon, Chris, *Beat Dyslexia*, LDA

Neanon, Chris (2002), *How to Identify and Support Children with Dyslexia*, LDA

Neanon, Chris, *Number Shark*, LDA

Neanon, Chris, *Word Shark*, LDA

O'Regan, F. (2002) *How to Teach and Manage Children with ADHD*, LDA

Portwood, Madeline (2000), *Understanding Developmental Dyspraxia: A textbook for students and professionals*, David Fulton

Portwood, Madeline, *Write from the Start, Speed up!* Writestart Desktop LDA

Thompson, G. (2003), *Supporting Communication Disorders: A handbook for teachers and teaching assistants*, David Fulton

Train, A. (1995), *The Bullying Problem*, Souvenir Press

Additional Resources

Attention Training Systems, GSI Publications Inc, PO Box 746, Dewitt NY 13214, USA (Tel. +00 315 446 4849; email addgsi@aol.com)

Further Reading on ADHD

Caffrey, J. (1997), *First Star I See*, Verbal Images Press

Gantos, J. (1998), *Joey Pigza Swallowed the Key*, Yearling Education

Green, C. (1997), *Understanding ADHD*, Doubleday Press

Kewley, G. (1999), *Recognition, Reality and Resolution*, LAC Press

Metcalf, J. and Metcalf, J. (2001), *Managing ADHD in the Inclusive Classroom*, David Fulton

SEN Organizations/Support Groups

ADDISS Information Services, tel. 0208 906 9068, www.addiss.co.uk

Afasic, tel. 0845 355 5577, www@afasic.org.uk

British Dyslexia Association, 98 London Road, Reading, Berkshire RG1 5AU, tel.
01189 668271, www.bda-dyslexia.org.uk

ADHD

Contact a Family, tel. 020 7608 8700, www.cafamily.org.uk
Dyslexia Institute, various locations, tel. 0178 4463851, www.dyslexia-inst.org.uk
Dyspraxia Foundation, 8 West Alley, Hitchin, Herts SG5 1EG, tel. 01462 454986
Hyperactive Children's Support Group, tel. 01243 551313, www.hacsg.org.uk
I CAN (organization for people with speech and language difficulties), tel. 0870 010 4066, email ican@ican.org.uk
National Austistic Society, tel. 0207 833 2299, email nas@nas.org.uk
National Association for Special Educational Needs (NASEN), tel. 01827 311500, www.nasen.org.uk
OAASIS (for people with autism/Asperger's), tel. 09068 633 3201